THE LOVE OF THE SUN

By the same author:

Surface (2004)
I Think We Have (2007)
angles of a broken hill (Ed.) (2008)
Eye to Eye (2012)
For Instance (2015)

THE LOVE OF THE SUN

MATT HETHERINGTON

RECENT
WORK
PRESS

The Love of the Sun
Recent Work Press
Canberra, Australia

Copyright © Matt Hetherington, 2018

ISBN: 9780648257936 (paperback)

 A catalogue record for this book is available from the National Library of Australia

All rights reserved. This book is copyright. Except for private study, research, criticism or reviews as permitted under the Copyright Act, no part of this book may be reproduced, stored in a retrieval system, or transmitted in any form by any means without prior written permission. Enquiries should be addressed to the publisher.

Cover design: Recent Work Press
Set by Recent Work Press
Author photograph by Brendan Bonsack

recentworkpress.com

For my twin-brother, Brett

Contents

A Poem Called	1
First Things	2
Soon Ago	3
Self-Portrait with Landscape	4
Estuary	5
Curtin	6
My Mother is Dead	7
Leave Me Alone	8
My Daughter at Sixty Months	9
Starving Girl, Calcutta	10
Bad Form	11
Page Poem	12
The Towers	13
Write It Softly	14
Moth Kisses	15
Standards	16
The Way to Stay as Dour as a Door All Day	17
Outlines	18
Heavy Petal	19
My Flat	20
The Anxiety of Affluence	21
Just	22
Don't Move On	23
In Not Of	24
We Had a Lovely Time	25
Pack of Lies	26
Temporary Like America	27
Sometimes I Wonder What's Going On	28
Dignity etc	29
Death Sentence	30
Guilt	31
Fade In	32

Free	33
Goes Without Saying	34
Mangoes	35
Escape	36
I Am Making	37
One or Two	38
Forest Storm	39
Broken Hill	40
After a Great Flood	41
No	42
YOU KNOW WHAT THIS IS	43
Recedes	44
Publisher: How to Hunt Writer	45
Chifley	46
Patient	47
Solitude	48
Mattina	49
Why I Am Not a Poet	50
Demands	51
There	52
There Again	53
Persistence	54
Flowers by the Roadside	55

The raging sea of fire out in space
is transformed to a caress.

Thomas Transtromer,
'The Light Streams In' (trans. Robin Fulton)

A Poem Called

left a message, it said just because you left
and said goodbye doesn't mean you're free
from the weight of younger things or because mess
ages that you shouldn't be afraid
of those with immaculate houses, now get
back to your homework, don't flatter yourself
and don't flatten yourself, perversity is the mother
of convention and there's always
never long to live, no pain, no gratitude
but your body will yell that, too
until you hear the echo first and you come from
where you're going by being a being being, bye now

First Things

already slightly light-headed from thirst
i go walking in the warming morning

the sun puts its arms around me
before i have even reached the gate

the city shimmers like a pale blue marble, and there's houses
among the trees, not trees among the houses

naturally, they make me think of the long length
of your strong brown limbs, and what they can do to me

we all want the same thing—you know what it is
we all breathe the same dehydrated rain

me, these days, i drink only six things—
beer, green tea, wine, coffee, water, and you

Soon Ago

After Emily Kngwarreye's 'Drying wildflowers'

we're here, so let's meet in the middle for as long as
the sun is warm and doesn't make a sound
no one's hiding anywhere, the air doesn't cover its face
and earth offers soft things so they skin-drink the day
these hands are as busy as flies but
hope you're not reading too fast
what's known, what's always shown, you can feel it
with seeds all around, no need to ask
what's the point of a circle? don't get stuck
like a stick in the muddy, the sky is in the ground

Self-Portrait with Landscape

important, but a bit odd, like a key-ring
with only one key, or an organ-grinder's
monkey, but not a chimp, really a sort
of browny-orangeish orangutan, picking
highly nutritious seeds out of its navel,
self-regard slow, but sure,
with the odd signal to colleagues

from a safe distance mostly, though
preferring to brood towards yet another
sky, which, like something ancient
for a change, is as gray as
a dying man's head, bending low
and stiff-tongued towards his lover
to scribble away the late-evening glow

Estuary

'I want to go back to being what I have not been'
Pablo Neruda, 'Oh Earth, Wait for Me'

the road is as long as the sky is wide
and the horizon is a hyphen between past and future

we stumbled through a forest of eyes to get here
just in time to watch a certain curtain fall

now the wind turns the green water silver
where the river gives its newness to the deep

this is when we are made to know the name of our face
and each of us comes to meet the rest

where we lie in a box of sleep

Curtin

it won't take long
the leaves will blow the past away
a little winter sun appears to melt the fog
dogs lead the way
and last night a farmer chased one
all across the sky
the light licks your ears
nameless flowers nod their heads
and all the paths lead home

My Mother is Dead

i'd had the first call
late in the morning.
my brother, the younger one
who i hardly talk to,
telling me 'you should get up here,
matt. she's really not good.'

i knew what it was
when the second call came.
i'd felt her go, ten minutes before
as i began the evening curry –

a small tug away from my chest,
like the last step of a long, formal dance.
the voice inside,
the one that gives me lines, said
'stirring the onions,
my mother is dead.'

Leave Me Alone

i don't care much about things
smaller than myself

or want much either
just real food from real soil

fruit & veg, lentils & rice
toast & honey, coffee & nuts

ok, warm sun & hot showers, too
a comfortable bed, a few people

& music, plus maybe
dry white wine & a banana lounge

where i can read endlessly
the good bad poetry

i also like to write

My Daughter at Sixty Months

For Jess

now she is at school.
though she still walks hand in hand with me, she strides through
   the schoolyard,
yelling greetings to her friends, who she has known for a few months.
she tells me the names of every one of the children in her class,
and i figure she'll be ok when they include *zifa, lily-rose,* and *satchmo.*

one of the few things that hasn't changed
is that her favourite dinner is still pasta, olives, and cheese,
but the only fruit she wants to eat lots of now is feijoas.
when she's excited or nervous or happy or bored
she clicks the fingers of both hands in a vaguely flamenco style.
she is a clever girl,
who truly knows better than me the meaning of 'never' and 'forever'.

she still talks a lot, occasionally teaching me phrases in italian,
or reminding me 'we are always outside'.
naturally, the questions continue, a couple of the latest being
'how are we made?' and 'why do we have to die?'
and in the last few weeks, she has used the words
'boyfriend', 'gun', and 'hate' for the first time.

a reasonable representation of our recent dialogues would be this one:
jess: 'my hand has disappeared!'
me: 'yeah, where's it gone?'
jess: 'the misery of nowhere.'

sounds ominously poetic, doesn't it?

Starving Girl, Calcutta

acting or not, it didn't matter
                she didn't need
                              to pretend
          to be desperate or debased or beyond despair
                what she was
                                  could not be hidden

i was only trying to leave the country
now trapped in the back of a taxi
                in a midday traffic jam
she clutched at me
                          through the open window
            sobbing, chanting, imploring, wailing
                        not even in english
(why didn't the driver do like he did with the others
                        and tell her to go get lost?)

i felt for coins but had none
so (keeping my notes for the next stage to the airport)
                as if it could help
                            i blessed her repeatedly

                    and for a whole two or three minutes
                              we stayed there
stuck in the spokes of the hideous, sacred wheel

                          at last the traffic moved forward
and she returned to her tribe under the plastic sheeting
while we drove upwards
                onto the rabindra setu bridge

Bad Form

punish it
      for being so unruly
discipline it
      if it won't be quiet in the middle of the night
teach it
      that a rule is a rule is a rule is a rule
cut it
    when it doesn't fit
hide it
      for being so plain to look at
deny it
    a home among the better forms
demonise it
      as 'the rotten apple that spoil it for the rest of us'
reprogramme it
   into an appropriate and functional model
categorise it
      so it knows where it belongs
publicise it
      as something 'extraordinary' and 'new'
sell it
   at a suitable profit
repeat it
   until the market has been saturated
kill it
    if you really want it dead

Page Poem

as soon as i see
it's small
i'm always already
a little fascinated

if it's quiet
like an insect
a liking
becomes a listening

but if it's obvious
in what it says
i escape by my fingertips

The Towers

they see
further than we do
& they frown down on us
they understand
what it is they do
& there are more every year

even inside, there is less
& less room
& one day
in a great suicide pact
they will all
topple over together

Write It Softly

the pleasure of lying in bed all morning
is worth so much more
than any amount of financial reward.
you are as warm as you wish,
as you try to remember your dreams,

or maybe you choose to lift your lids
to let the sunlight come in,
or to see the rain stay outside.
if you want, there are books and books and books,
or if hungry, some fresh fruit and nuts.

out there is work, most of it unnecessary,
or in lands much more poor than ours,
maybe a matter of death or life.
but here, where we are,
there is the ease of being still within the breath,

and i'm writing this lying in bed.

Moth Kisses

put your mouth
to mine
as if you're seeking the mother
of all silent love

we are slowly becoming ashes
but we want the growth of being burnt

you believe
you believe you see my eyes
yes
but close your lashes
and a deeper light
is exposed in your interior black room
where the softest red gently moves itself

strike a match and tell me
the air is not on fire

now part your lips
let me fly into you

Standards

my way
is testing

nature boy
gets lost

body and
soul inseparable

what's new
ain't desire

all blues
go grey

only you
own you

The Way to Stay as Dour as a Door All Day

It's really all about getting out of it, but on the inside only. Don't even think about bouncing beach-balls, even though now you're on permanent holiday, and you're so damn urbane you will never shout again. Convince yourself there's a sneeze ricocheting around the back of your head, and there's a bit of a warm breeze drifting in from the two o'clock snooze area for the other convalescents. Recall all those moonlit hours you worked to keep from falling asleep. Imagine the screen is your best pal, and the coffee-pot is calling you by name. Your boss is talking about giving up smoking again, you feel like a minister's wife, and you really, really want to yawn, and, gee, you must have permission, because even babies do it, but no, you mustn't. Even though that guy Ken is your friend, and you're staring at a plate of raw kale, don't. You're a loner. Don't forget it. Just don't act like a weird drifter-type, ok? They're always looking in windows, but you're not a window, are you? Windows are pushovers. Remember your ancestors. You're not stuck on a fishing boat for a week, you're not remembering every black and white morning of your life or moaning about being a panther in a zoo, ok, so shut it. Is the wind heavy? No. You're a bit slow, but I think you've got it now. It also helps to give up on love.

Outlines

'Days of peace, days of living velvet
H.P. Lovecraft

the distant hills like her body
lying on its side

the warm waters
pulsing beneath you

then the soft forest below
the long peak of your nose

& the cliff-face of your chin
resting on a green carpet-floor

a form above your heart
plays with endless hunger

& again the taste after embraces
returns you to the tongue

the body's strongest muscle

Heavy Petal

sitting on a road
a silence that can never be loud enough
after the beach each wave returns to the mother

the body remembers what the mind forgets
as naked as a splinter
you keep lapping at it with your fingers

writing in order to listen better
a depth-change
mouths arranged until they don't fit perfectly

born beautiful
easily distracted
a great deal more laughter required

a fan inside the flames
pain in the mirror of night
in mid-winter they warmed the room with hunger for more love

the wolves' paws, soft like blankets
the little trained ones don't need leads
act as if you are cared for

all day felt
as if behind rainy windows
navigating the void like grief was a ballast

in a while we will be elsewhere

My Flat

For Jennifer Allen

i don't go crazy
these days yet a dog barks a lot
sometimes at night & it's new
but birds can often be heard also

the big doors close
quite easily though the window's a little stiff
all flooring is now almost free of waterlogging
& the walls nearly gone of upmarket pet-marks

natural southern light abounds
in winter while transport & shopping is close
the neighbours keep their distance
& the garbage goes where it should

if you want to
you can nearly touch my ceilings
on odd occasions fallen crumbs may be left
the ants express interest also the rats

The Anxiety of Affluence

can't hide the tired beard, or unknow?
                      what you've seen, absolutely?
flat out screening, yes?
                it takes as much as it gives?
     even though all five walls are never quite right?
but you're not as guilty as the guillotine in your head?
             no one will
suit up for the argument or intimidate the witness?
replay the footage from the land of rumbling stomachs?

        truth is hollow like a shudder

every day that clever voice, it tells itself?
                    don't be aware, be alert?
           not to feel freedom's easiness?
what can you do
              it's like stabbing knives?
         you're a good man chained to command?
this proud business, shifting digits?
                  it makes you laugh all over?
      your eyes are as blank as a bank?

Just

nothing interests me less
all those oiled parts
lying at the desk
than failing to dissemble

no-one wants to see
a pear-shaped balloon
or two triangles wrestling
let alone those talking

being where i am
then words may remain
doors once were trees
with hunger for water

just let me live
the triumph of air
love is the hand
to see past pasts

than their secret dreams
and brief family holidays
is so much easier
before the knowing eyes

a clown letting go
squeezed at the waist
with each other's points
to keep from thinking

i'm where i be
like old wood should
trees were once seeds
and thirst for fire

the miracle of blood
and death's great night
freed by the glove
to learn beyond life

Don't Move On

drifting in
to be where you need
to find a shiny puddle
of ill-will
for examining your grimace in

seeing you
are like all the rest
but the invisible finger-prints of love
on your face
are yours alone

alone

you return to the surfaces

In Not Of

it's raining in our brains and on the streets;
black clouds make themselves at home in the ground.
the publican, too, can't wait to get a drink in him,
though first he tells me, "all the trees say 'Y',
but the soil can only answer 'yes'."
you want to ask what life is for, but you know already
you won't know until you've seen
behind the shadow under the barred-up exit door.

mate, i went there to escape the war of the exes, mate,
and with all the manners of a mosquito,
i ordered before i was hungry, but still i ate.
not much to it, really, but potatoes and meat
with a hint of a thousand islands,
though of course tomorrow it could be winter again.

We Had a Lovely Time

we laughed at nothing
until we couldn't stand up
we synchronized our watches
then crushed them in our eye-sockets

i fed her child milk
until he could walk along fences
we made the horizon
break into a smile

i cut a slice off the moon
and put it in her drink
she tickled me with blinks
until i begged to be untied

we travelled to a land where the beggars had no hands
and we applauded them
i put a sprig of parsley in her belly button
then i ate her stomach

we kept our love in a box
then we took it to the forest and set it free
and then we slept so long
our limbs grew together

i gave her this poem
and she finished it

Pack of Lies

you couldn't get it
through the door
it was so full
of itself
or some stuff
i don't get
'cos it's so shiny it's
blinding
like love or something
i don't get either
and it was naturally
express post
or some such
unnatural thing
with a stamp of the queen
of some dying country
you can't get to
without a lot of cash
plus it was warped like
an old present
from someone
you managed to forget
and i even had to
sign for it

Temporary Like America

it doesn't rhyme with miracle
or austria or shit or luck or failure
it's as lonesome as a guitar with only one string

oh my lil ol' bittersweet juice-sucker
through the racket of your brave sad gladness
hear me typing to ya

and i have to tell you that you did wrong
and cos you haven't learnt to dig yuhself
you're as likely to say sorry as a baby, baby

you can deny it later
and pay for it in neverland
when you're as empty inside as a dead cop's wallet

everybody knows america is everywhere
but not everyone knows this is nowhere
and you're like totally like not

not hot not cool not here not there
a simpering goddess sipping gossip
but just before you die
you will suddenly be very young

Sometimes I Wonder What's Going On

she turns up wanting space
she's not wearing green again
why aren't her kids making her happy?

she wants to up her dosage to where it was
before she cancelled the ceremony
she needs to start smoking again
but her mother has just given up

she can't remember what she forgot
she has a different voice for everyone she knows

someone dedicated a book to her
but she was smarter and never read it
she's like an avocado inside-out

she likes to renovate her hair
her brain is like a magazine
she apologises but can't tell you why

while she's smoking a joint, she tells you
you're the only thing wrong with her life
she doesn't see
it's going to burn her
and you don't tell her

Dignity etc

i listen to something
gone cute on my heart again
a few simple words like
the dog jumps over the trapdoor spider
or the thin woman is flabbergasted
or the racist eats a banana
maybe it was really the shudder
of someone dodging a coffin
still the cows keep chewing their grass
the locks stay pretty well locked
the days go past like bees
and everyone puts their feet on the seats

Death Sentence

'Roger Gilbert-Lecomte...proclaims that human beings are in the process of turning into *insects*. He allows that, consistent with this mutation, men will become so busy that they will lose their ability to dream...'
Philip Beitchman, *I Am a Process with No Subject*

no two webs are exactly identical
yet we good citizens become increasingly alike

as we proceed in straight lines
towards each carefully glistening task

& we rub our limbs up & down
while our eyes grow ever larger

& we hum with the intent of our instructions
until we suddenly find ourselves stuck

in mid-transit—

but the more quietly we struggle
the more we call

the patience of the spider

Guilt

by the time they woke
the sun was gone
night had fallen
in love with itself
they were breathing
dust and hoarding numbers
be quiet
i already told you
they will
not survive

Fade In

you have committed a terrible crime.
for part of the year the clouds drop a little pale rain,
and half the time you cringe as if you're past the end,
trapped in this city without seasons.

you churn on through the streets, camouflaged in black,
mad with fatigue and pouring fire onto fire.
you meet, then part, tied to the moon like tides.
all day the sky returns your stare.

the wish to be ambitionless grooms itself,
but really, you're only washing mud off with blood.
see – your friends are waving goodbye to the trees,
and now even grief leaves you alone.

Free

you say you
won't go down
with your tears
but rise up
with your eyebrows

you can't believe
a single drop
since you're alone
enough to give
your old heart
the third degree
but never burn

space must exist
for precisely this
knowing your roots
as being at
absolute rock bottom

Goes Without Saying

love is a fly you can't kill
even with a literary work

as usual, grey matter was blocking the sun
and wet winds muttered underneath their breath

every morning
she put words in his mouth he couldn't swallow
every night
he wrapped his arms around her like a shroud

at times, the child got between their lips
something ugly was scowling from the glass

the moral of this story is
always put styles before substances

so when will i see you again?

Mangoes

inside
fruit shops
he finds them
waiting there takes
as many as he has
money for bites into
each skin and tears off
with nails and then teeth
the flesh is like sun
inside his tongue

Escape

For Luce

it's pretty funny, i'm happiest
lying on my left-hand side
reading or writing
with my old right hand
or stroking the back of my love

the front appears
to have been created for tasting
so i cease my speech
and drink in anything
that seems not to be myself

still, when it's at its most free
i feel like i'm dancing inside
on all three levels at once
of the capital 'E'
in 'SHE' or 'HE' or 'WE'

I Am Making

i am making a present for you
                              it is myself
        i am making myself
    into something worth giving to you

if i ever finish
                        i will take paper
            from my old books
and you can wrap me up in it

                              or yourself

One or Two

i like to be with one or two people.
one is best, and that one is me.

one or two times i was in love.
well, they're the ones i admit to.

one or two adults will grow up
and have one or two kids.

one or two souls behave
as if we're really all one soul.

one or two old pains are better
than one or two new ones.

one or two days a year
the show doesn't go on.

one or two times
can sometimes be an understatement.

one or two people are usually right,
especially when they agree with me.

one or two techniques exist
for uncovering one's heart.

one or two people will keep on
reading all the way to the end.

Forest Storm

my best friend in my head said 'you're not
dead yet.' so now i'm well
i'm rising to bells, as greedy as the world

we stand as though we'd never known a tower
but help us all, we think we're stalling
where roads open out onto flowing fields of rain
and grain bends towards the darkness
of its mother and father and its calling

lean trees like me lean north, but the truth is
headed west into the desert, where it throbs all day
like non-occurring dreams

limbs are falling all around us
and the wind is pulling its own hair
the dead aren't in the air, they're here

Broken Hill

when i leave i hope
i will carry the spirits on my skin
i will carry the earth in my legs
the sky in my eyes

when i leave i hope
i will carry the birds in my feet
the trees in my shoulders
the people in my chest

when i leave i hope
i will carry the stars in my fingers
the breeze on my eyelashes
the sunset in my forehead

when i leave i hope
i will carry the dark in my arms
the sun in my spine
i will carry the silence in my blood

when i return i hope
i will forget what i have carried

After a Great Flood

Uki, NSW, April 1, 2017

        dirt everywhere, no electricity,
no mobile phone reception, and no clean water.

roads with large chunks missing,
                trees and signs lying down.

      a distinct lack of birds, but louder frogs,
strangers talking to each other.

already there are piles of rubbish roughly stacked,
and your eternal, aphoristic, internal critic reciting

    'be on, if you want to
    be beyond.'

No

maybe we're all   still in chains   but it's okay
to know comfort   is not that   far away today

we fool around   like no tomorrow   but it's good
to not talk   or even think   about our history

anyway let's drink   to our leaders   and hidden law-makers
who couldn't take   enough from all   that wasn't theirs

YOU KNOW WHAT THIS IS

< > rushing at your face like wind < >
               < > there's a new moon coming soon < >
               < > trees shaking their fists < >
< > the sky like a misted-up window < >
    < > every car is a hearse < >
    < > spiders climbing down from their webs < >
         < > a stamp left on your eyes < >
               < > babies in the sewers < >
                     < > your fingers typing
in your sleep <>
< > all the legends begging to be shot < >
       < > a faint taste of sperm in the air < >

Recedes

one more eyeball implodes.

from a warm cave
she asked about a word
then offered me her lips.

we lay down on a platform up high,
and sun almost came into the winter
that was living under all those black heads.

what feels wrong to you?

i know.
double chins are everywhere.
hands aren't free.

spain is fairly close to germany.

Publisher: How to Hunt Writer

After Dan Disney

Take hole for writer to climb out of, and casually enter urban jungle / bohemian enclave. Arrange suitable darkness, electric moons, mirrors, and other vanity items. Call your zookeeper buddies. Shave head, if not already bald. Smear yourself in mousefat. Wait. While waiting, make more calls. Have picture taken with local savages. Say 'cheese'. Without irony. Appreciate local dances. Always take weekend off. When questioned, only give answers as products. Smile. Wait more—the shy ones are best. While waiting, always talk. Especially about the power of silence. Or whether to laugh or not. Do not take mescalin. Take ecstasy at aforementioned local dances. Focus on maintaining loss of control. Smile. The reasonably shy ones should be watching now. Scare them away with accountants. Do not quote Machiavelli, Sartre, or Jane Bowles publicly. Do not mention pubic hair. Cultivate three-day growth and taste for crackers. Say 'cheese'. Love your enemy well. Stay down-wind of your own nose. Try to feel sadness. Or empathy. Or something. This will bring true naïve-child-beast genius out of (real) hole. Make sure writer / genius is very ugly or very beautiful. Gaze dully like mule. Become mule. Accidentally eat writer. Start again or retire.

Chifley

it's not too far to the shops
and you can suck
on laneway honeysuckle on the way
jeez, music means you can't
sit still, and i promise the look
on my face isn't mine, but like a book
i've got my own jacket
i know that's not a spider
but here come the galloping fingers

Patient

my mother died holding
my twin-brother's hand

as sometimes happens
i was a day late to see

he knew, too
when she left

because the machine
beside her

displayed the words
'DISCONNECT PATIENT'

Solitude

let me hear you sing, people
        who need people are the loneliest people in the world
though two of every animalistic urge
        seems about right before the deluge
they dry us out
        but the rains will pass like extensive shivers
inside, the never-ending present
        a warm bath and a firm bed
            outside, scaffolds and rags and detours

        when your tongue is overgrown with rust
    truth is wasted on the old, but it's a dancing
point between spheres, and you are everything
            you can be
                a weeping mirror of joy

Mattina

After Giuseppe Ungaretti

i

lie

in

a

bed

which

lies

in

a

bath

of

light

Why I Am Not a Poet

they want to be first & last
but not the best or worst

their magic consists of nothing but turning
blood into words and mud into water

their hearts are made of sand
and smell like sardines

their souls are like tar mixed with flowers
they know the worth of instants but not of hours

they write better when they don't think
& whine better when they drink

they write for themselves
then someone or other

for them, the sky can be orange & the sun blue
and everything's not what it isn't

they laugh at the tragic and smile at the funny
poets are the neediest & greediest

but not for love or money

Demands

crumple up the mountains, leave
as if it's a competition in kindness

yet again we're letting the fruit rot
and our fear is as clear and near as a mirror

your hands are becoming cheap paper
and already there are ghosts buried in the desert

now count the counters turning over into hours
as softly as the sun summersaults over the cow

sure, you're good to wood like a placemat
but how many times can you ask the same question?

    the land demands answers, so tell yourself
    you can hear yourself another time

    and before you arrive
    wrap your tongue with wire

There

'just rapture & despair,
between them, longing'
Paul Summers, 'dasein'

   i wanted you like i want to chew
the warm, ordinary town that brought me you
to savour it like saltiness, & spit it out into the night
        like you yearn to be liquidity
                dissolving into soil
     like we don't want to hide
     like no one wants to hold what they can't bear to see

infinite sister, who wants to be straight?
                no tree is perfectly that way
   your eyes are melting dark
        & down there, you taste the way corn-silk does
so let me enter the centre of the heart of your heart
        or i will leave, & going
            kiss the lucid fragrance of your filthy feet

There Again

After Robert Brownhall's 'Night arrows'

nothing is burning is overlooked
like glass the sky is not a limit is time
to pay our last respects to the present
now where is tedium it's not what was left
behind all the questions pushing it uphill is not
the end of the road or home where you don't think it
should have been no signs won't be blanker than mirrors
though how many yawns from dusk to dawn all sleep falls
into it but no fighting in the alleys now no reason to hide no faces
everywhere you don't turn just to be on the safe side it says the forbidden is not
hidden like green fire in all the miles of smiles the one with the quietest voice wins

Persistence

i drank away
the hangover
and the green tea
went down
like warm autumn rain

ah the day
and the hours
when the light is within all things
and the sweetness of tears
comes easily

then it is good
to have a simple dinner
of soup and bread
and to go to bed early
having achieved nothing

Flowers by the Roadside

nights full of days
      days full of the night

& in the hour in between
        looking to the clock a lot

            the bottle stands to attention
        you salute yourself

          ignoring the warning
                a peak like the beak of a crow

        the winds turn through the hills
the ways undo themselves

            we always went so fast
      wanting too much to be

    what we were
more than all

Afterword

Things such as these were inside me during the writing of this book:

'It is through reverence that the work, always already in ruins, is frozen: through reverence which prolongs, maintains, consecrates it (through the idolatry proper to titles), it congeals, or is added to the catalogue of the good works of culture.'
Maurice Blanchot, *The Writing of the Disaster*

'But metaphors are transformations, proofs of the arbitrary nature of language, grants of mystery to ordinary things – they are in other words incipient utopias.'
Greil Marcus, *Lipstick Traces*

'There's a very thin line that separates the strong, true, bright bird of the imagination from the synthetic, noisy bauble.'
Arundhati Roy, 'The Ladies Have Feelings, So...'

'...the possibility that this extraordinary eye would really come to light through the bony roof of the head, because I believed it necessary that, after a long period of servility, human beings would have an eye just for the sun...'
Georges Bataille, 'The Jesuve'

'The falsest manners of speaking are the most entertaining, as long as there are people who use them earnestly.'
Elias Canetti, *The Human Province*

'(Thomas Mann) once said that all his work could be understood as an effort to free himself from the middle class, and this...will serve to describe the chief intention of modern literature."
Lionel Trilling, 'Of the Teaching of Modern Literature'

'Even before reason there is the inward movement which reaches out towards its own.'
Plotinus, *Enneads*.

'The organ of sight begins by being a source of light. The eye is a lamp. It doesn't receive light, it gives it.'
Jacques Derrida, *The Gift of Death*

'November 4. Blinded by the sun of my own longing to see.'
Olivia Dresher, 'Moments and Confessions 2002'

'Leisure would soon be the axis of civilization: a realm of potential happiness so complete that it would test the power of all the mechanisms of alienation to dominate it. [...] If leisure were conquered, civilization would turn into a prison disguised as a pleasure dome. But if leisure was not conquered, it would serve as a base for a practice of freedom so explosive that no known social order could ever satisfy it.'
Greil Marcus, *Lipstick Traces*

'Neither the sun, nor the universe helps us, except through images, to conceive of a system of exchanges so marked by loss that nothing therein would hold together and that the inexchangeable would no longer be caught and defined in symbolic terms. (...) The cosmic reassures us, for we can identify with the measureless vibration of a sovereign order even if in this identification we venture beyond ourselves, entrusting ourselves to a holy and real unity. So it is with being and probably with all ontology.'
Maurice Blanchot, *The Writing of the Disaster*

Acknowledgements

My thanks to the many editors who published a number of these poems (some in earlier forms) in the following publications, e-zines, and anthologies:

&; Abridged (NIR)Bareknuckle Poet ; The Best Australian Poetry 2007; Best Australian Poems 2012; Best Australian Poems 2014; Blue Dog; The Canberra Times; Cordite; Cottonmouth; Divan; fourW ; From This Broken Hill; Furiously Knocking; Husk; INSCRIBE; Lentil Republic; Letters to the A.C.T; Malleable Jangle; Mascara Literary Review; Melaleuca; The Mini-Mag (USA); neither/nor; Otoliths; Peril; Plumwood Mountain Journal; Pressure Gauge Press; Searching for the Sublime; Stillcraic; Social Alternatives; Southerly; Speedpoets; Teesta (IND); Tincture; Trope; Verge; Verity La; VLAK (CZE)

A number of these poems have been broadcast on the television show Red Lobster (Channel31), and on the radio shows *badslampoetryblog* (2XX) and *Spoken Word* (3CR).

Sun-sized thanks to Shane Strange for his work on this and all the other poetry collections he's been involved with, and to Ali Alizadeh, Stuart Barnes, Brett Hetherington, and Melinda Smith, who all read much longer versions of this book, then supplied much-valued critique. My long-standing gratitude also goes to those who have helped with my writing during this time, particularly Grant Caldwell, Coral Carter, Jennifer Compton, Nola Firth, Lia Hills, Andy Jackson, Myron Lysenko, Ian McBryde, Simon Munro, Nathan Shepherdson, David Stavanger, Patrick Ulrich, Annie Te Whiu, and Benjamin Wild.

Thanks to the Wheeler Centre, Melbourne, and their assistance in the writing of this book with a 'Hot Desk' Fellowship through Melbourne P.E.N in 2012.

Matt Hetherington is a writer, music-maker, teacher, part-time DJ, and moderate self-promoter based in northern New South Wales. He has been reading his poetry in public regularly since 1995, and was co-editor of *Straight from the Tank,* a documentary film featuring over 60 poetry performances in Melbourne from 2003-2005. He has translated poetry from French and Spanish, as well as the Turkish of Hidayet Ceylan, and he is also on the board of the Australian Haiku Society. Some current inspirations are: Tristan Tzara, Pep Guardiola, and black sesame. This is his fifth poetry collection.

2018 Editions

The Uncommon Feast **Eileen Chong**
Inlandia **KA Nelson**
Peripheral Vision **Martin Dolan**
Cavorting with Time **Jacqui Malins** and **Caren Florance**
The Love of the Sun **Matt Hetherington**
Ley Lines and the Rustling of Cedar **Niloofar Fanaiyan**
Things I've Thought to Tell You Since I Saw You Last **Penelope Layland**
Moving Targets **Jen Webb**
The Many Uses of Mint **Ravi Shankar**
Abstractions **Various**

2017 Editions

A Song, the World to Come **Miranda Lello**
Cities: Ten Poets, Ten Cities **Various**
The Bulmer Murder **Paul Munden**
Dew and Broken Glass **Penny Drysdale**
Members Only **Melinda Smith** and **Caren Florance**
the future, un-imagine **Angela Gardner** and **Caren Florance**
Proof **Maggie Shapley**
Black Tulips **Moya Pacey**
Soap **Charlotte Guest**
Isolator **Monica Carroll**
Ikaros **Paul Hetherington**
Work & Play **Owen Bullock**

all titles available from
www.recentworkpress.com

www.ingramcontent.com/pod-product-compliance
Lightning Source LLC
Chambersburg PA
CBHW032049290426
44110CB00012B/1023